Cherrystem

poems by

Alison Moncrieff

Finishing Line Press
Georgetown, Kentucky

Cherrystem

for Mom

Copyright © 2017 by author Alison Moncrieff
ISBN 978-1-63534-169-0 First Edition
All rights reserved under International and Pan-American Copyright Conventions. No part of this book may be reproduced in any manner whatsoever without written permission from the publisher, except in the case of brief quotations embodied in critical articles and reviews.

ACKNOWLEDGMENTS

"clotho" and "Y" first appeared in *Rivet Journal*. Thank you to Red Bridge Press.

Thank you to Dave Nash for sharing my life and saying *yes* so much. To Ian & Nora for being yourselves and my kindest teachers. To Robert Moncrieff, Diane Moncrieff, and Scott Moncrieff for your lifelong love and support. To Sandra Wong-Orloff for your friendship and for letting me put "Balancing" on the cover of this book. To Susan Leahy for your friendship and fun. To Elizabeth Treadwell for reminding me about poetry. To Mary Loughran for asking me to read with you at Bay Area Generations. To Paul Corman-Roberts for inviting me to read that time at Passages on the Lake and for being a giant-hearted force for poetry folk. To Jan Steckel for being inspiring and demonstrating how to own a room. To Amos White for reading this manuscript first. To Wendy Snyder for moving to the neighborhood. To David Pedersen for generally being a champion of me. To Fred Dodsworth for your kind energy. To Liz Walker for helping me find my own way. To all the local poets who read out and who have moved me beyond myself in the temple of words. <3

Publisher: Leah Maines
Editor: Christen Kincaid
Cover Art: Sandra Wong-Orloff/Artist
Author Photo: Alison Moncrieff
Cover Design: Elizabeth Maines McCleavy

Printed in the USA on acid-free paper.
Order online: www.finishinglinepress.com
also available on amazon.com

Author inquiries and mail orders:
Finishing Line Press
P. O. Box 1626
Georgetown, Kentucky 40324
U. S. A.

Table of Contents

i will never 1
kiddo 2
net 3
junjie explains things to trixie 4
pony 5
diastasis recti *6*
sekhmet 7
estudillo avenue 8
sanctuary 9
poppet 10
blodison *11*
blood moon 12
featured artist 13
clairaudience 14
sunol 15
what passes for pretty 16
into it 17
sough 18
clotho 19
let 20
lunatic 21
Y 22
motorcycle 23
we can be us   *for david bowie* 24
exoneration 25

y'all's projection of maternal
purity of heart

i will never

pin down a house & pieces
a 2-way mirror between worlds
in what temperament
i didn't really enjoy being
shoved into figures of authority
while stoned make sense of your life
that clique at school & by the way
history isn't the only thing
to feel attractive ran through
the greenhouse uprooting plants

kiddo

seems everything in
this world is about the body
my teenage dream: the corpse of someone
i killed & buried
a happy hound
at my original vagina
all the ways i walked
to school not knowing
the strap language of adolescence

net

structurally if strong
as tulle tho bulky
a net for stalking prey
in shallow waters i ret you down
you stomp you net yourself
strung up between the poles
sag your sinking skin
caught in a knotted history
i ret you down you twist
you mud yourself
filthlinking to every
diggy little elbow point
all sinewy all shiny
was the chevy hood
see thru places where
you flip reflection
through tutu and tulle to
better worlds than yours

junjie explains things to trixie

ghouled by dark water
bluster is fight
twist your precious elementals
burps & goon bludgeon
& stinky bugs ideas
ghouling the elementals
darkbane & redhook
a premonition a dream
shadow clan transforms
the messer the enigmo

pony

meeting minty & twilight
sparkle in a hospital bed
a penny in your throat
talents & cutie marks
a candybox of registers
toward knowing
your selfied insides

diastasis recti

charmsewn, hopefully
fire-edged abdominals
singed deckles standing off chapter after chapter
until their plotlines expire
they flare at any attempt to rebind
they have their own lives now
spin-offs I can't follow

on some social media site
a woman posted a photo of her abdomen after kids
an anonymous confession of grit and pride
her belly stretched & softly hanging
like mine like a popped balloon
she was wearing low rise jeans and a leather biker belt
she stood behind it like we do
her face was not in the photo
just her sacred garment, her engaged skin
documenting that singular odyssey to motherhero

however our children get into the world

anyway, there's a chakra
in there somewhere and a Latin name
that sounds like *diaphanous necktie*

in the book, turn to page 37
see our spines shining out
between signatures

sekhmet

multitudes in me
the pharaoh's salve & suture
my solar disk inscribes a fire line
around your path to victory
i breathe a desert
inhale your ailing lung
stricken by me
i blow it back new

estudillo avenue

it's no less real
oh funerary sirens
to see you in my trances
the crowded hospital
estudillo avenue &
a child sleeping under snow
abides the lonely motorcycle
a fallen tower card a tablo

sanctuary

of dying beds & labyrinths
made of lawn an alley wall
holds some perfect interchange
the air the leaves are wet with you
lit bright with you and you and you
the world an altared thing

poppet

the littlest one made a doll of you
construction paper, marker, tape
she made more: with toilet paper & string;
with sticks bound together, caped in dimity
grass for hair. she grasps them
with both hands, caresses them
to conjure joy for you
now a goddess up in the sky

blodison

a blessing's root is in our veins
whether we believe
forget the body
its consecrations & star quality
whether marked or hallowed
all over the old altars
or coursing a bliss
of messed up meaning
speak however of us

blood moon

russet eye
of a pulse of a hole
bearing something loving
if not the end of the world
this bistered minute
then a candy dot for jesus
in the sugar window
unclot to spatter a floating lens
the shot field glasses
cracked claim to have written
a brief but bestselling self care primer
while standing on her daughter's bed
craning to some sensational shadow
of a pill of a pulse

featured artist

blown up script
mothers dredging recipes
all bound up in the living world
the future's goodwill endcaps
feathered with snips
of talk of family dinners
voices all wings
freed up from audio
from i feel a century
its bloods and subjugations
how the terminal scratch & pick
at dimensional walls where
you hang yourself until

clairaudience

hawk & owl gliding
over marrow praying
how your daddy lit fires
at sundown fathoming
by vital timbre : bones & dawn
hemming his feathered ear
i don't have to hate the sorrow
of losing you a certain bird
says *spirit*, a natural jingle of the dead
on quiet beaming tongues
exhales the sun, swims to sit
on the bottom of the sky

sunol

as the life of a squirrel sowing
rock ribbons the green bodice
featherbone banderole
as the life of a day shadowing
bay blue oak raised rib
a sycamore king
as the life of a snake ruling
the lunch basket
elderberry white alder
as the life of a cicada emerging
lichen moss a lupine
mountain calving off
chance and anonymous
as the life of a squirrel sowing

what passes for pretty

in a lit world
a field of electric light
smashing darkness
pressing & damping
an underlife an indexed petite
how foul the rack
besting the yetis leaving no footprint
ahoy, dePenis Canting
sing something different
bare tendril how bleak your itinerary
a wonder cracked cold

into it

arch deterioration
forsake a draft
of self-marked avenues
to psyche & statuary
a scripture you
are rarely around it's
understated DIY
trepanation this time of night
of fluted homespun brains
of pinking shears
this musselled corner
a hole-punch mourning
our capsule our coasts

sough

weightless the afterlife afterthought
hush way below the sparkle of the sea
harness salt to move our heat around
brew magical acids from muscle & milk
we will live further down before dying tho
the brine pool's concentration can't beat
the licks and salines of a pastoral life biting
blades to the soil at moondown we rise
to the sough of the sea our blanket woven
with worm mussel mud-volcano clam
a mystical number back in our brains recalls
the sun will travel through time recalls
the starshine will travel through time recalls
a split in the earthcore speaking light

clotho

there can be no revival of the form

who foraged fiber
twisted it up like a weed
from the ocean floor
feasted with the others
on the life it fastened

who could have the idea
being idea
to interfere while twirling
mermaid silk with distaff tending
a mythical string into life

whose seagrass field is fading
a plastic cup hovers
over the ocean floor
it is your sister's job to weave

let

this too is strung
topspun & intended
or a service to the alley
a let begets a hold

lunatic

& healing wired
a burgeon to hide
witch-hazy feed
your fingers in
divine me darkest
unlit spheres
labile sound
divine me lucid
fully & lunatic the flairy
mess & medical water
adolescences scaping
beach to brussels
fielding coastlines
with pleasure an arm
up from the waves
of my cloth

Y

rustine, the undersqueak of your carriage
i seen your bed rustin' in the yard
milkweed growing all up in its frame
parts of you rise up between hunks of the old hiway
rain tools the weedpath in wishbones, sugar
split your selves crazy, that's what you did
same way a road cherrystems into wilderness

motorcycle

part our waters
clear that split-lane skim
a beeswarm motor pulse
past ambulance down threnody
thru glowing leaf & lens

a glassway back
to an animal passing
inside our hiway glade

we can be us *for david bowie*

just be still with me
here where we've been
a quagmire forming in the yard
you are all overwrought & sweaty
pondering the superstition of your identity

exoneration

our story's in the thing
behind this patterned broadcast

Growing up in northern California, **Alison Moncrieff** spent long periods time outside playing with friends, reading, and collecting materials from the natural world. Back then, she wanted to be an archeologist and her hero was Dr. L. S. B. Leakey. When she was inside, she played Pong, sewed clothing and cooked with her mom, and watched TV shows like *Wild Wild West, Wild Kingdom, Mr. Ed,* and anything that featured Dr. Leakey. She also wanted to be a novelist and tried, at first, to write her own books by copying other people's. She studied English and creative writing at Mills College in the late 80s after which time she did not write for many years. While working in a local bookstore, she created a non-fiction section entitled "Visitations" which featured books about aliens visiting Earth. Among other occupations, she was a writer for the National Park Service, a lingerie fitter for women with prosthetic breasts, a computer book editor, and a garden designer. A homeschooling mom as well as a writer, she lives in Oakland, California with her husband, 2 children, and 13 animals.

www.ingramcontent.com/pod-product-compliance
Lightning Source LLC
LaVergne TN
LVHW041515070426
835507LV00012B/1588